Mean Cat by Melanie Gidget Anderson

Mean Cat by Melanie Gidget Adams

Mean Cat

By Melanie (Gidget) Adams

Mean Cat by Melanie Gidget Adams

Acknowledgements

Photos on Front Cover and On Page 6:
Valerie Holloway
My sister, and an outstanding photographer!

Photo on Page 19: Bill Runk
A wonderful friend, and awesome photographer!

Photos and Designs on Pages 21-25:
*Are credited to their respective owners and
I would recommend any of them!*

Images of "Great Toys" on Page 37: Belong to their
respective owners as well and I have no claims
pertaining the photography or the invention of
these toys... I just think they're great!

All other photos were taken by me, the author:
Melanie (Gidget) Adams

Proofreading Credit: Ethan Jones
My great nephew, a very confident young man!
He and his little sister Emmy are the
greatest kids on the planet!

Supportive Family Members:
Miss. Linda (my Loving Mother)
Monte Holloway - Melanie Jones
And Everyone Listed Above

Many Thanks, to All of You!

Mean Cat by Melanie Gidget Adams

In Loving Memory of Louie
- and eleven years of battle scars -

Mean Cat by Melanie Gidget Adams

INTRODUCTION

Born on the bayou (and with a lot of attitude), Louie was a mean little "Cajun Kitty". He was so tiny, so cute, and he was a welcome addition to our home in Louisiana. We (my mother and I) actually thought it was funny that he was already biting people at such a young age. When we realized he wasn't growing out of it though (as he added *scratching* to his abuse, we knew we had a little monster on our hands.

* *

I would like to share with you the hard lessons I've learned by not obtaining the knowledge, and the skills Needed to help Louie. He lived nearly his entire life angry at the world and we never knew why.. or that there even *was* a reason. Looking back now, and after raising a few other cats in his wake, we learned a great deal about what makes a cat tick, and what ticks off a cat.

To resolve the problems you're having with your cat, you first need to understand the reasons for his lashing out. Before you can make any plans to take action, you may want to utilize this guide to figure out what's going on with him. Once you have figured it out, continue reading for solutions pertaining to your cat's specific problems.

1

Mean Cat by Melanie Gidget Adams

TABLE OF CONTENTS

Mean Cat by Melanie Gidget Adams

WHAT MAKES A CAT MEAN

In order to calm your cat, you need to figure out why he is unhappy, and consequently, making you unhappy. Below, are some possible reasons your cat is acting out:

- Kitty has a medical problem and may be in pain.
- It is possible that your cat is stressed, maybe even insecure.
- Maybe your cat is being bullied by another animal or person.
- Maybe your cat is feeling neglected, and needs some loving attention.
- Kitty may sense a threat that you are not aware of.
- It is possible your cat does not like the way you touch him.
- Maybe because of your cat's breed, he needs special adjustments to be made.
- Maybe kitty needs a sanctuary or a safe place to hide.

FERAL, STRAY, & DOMESTICATED CATS

As you probably already know, there are significant distinctions between feral, stray, and domesticated cats. It's important to know whether or not you are dealing with a *wild* feline, or just a mean house cat:

FERAL: Completely wild, and difficult to tame.

STRAY: Had a home but left, or was dumped.

DOMESTICATED: Has always lived with people.

BEHAVIORS OF A MEAN CAT

It is pretty easy to tell if your cat is mean, and not just a typical ornery type. The most common behaviors of a cat with serious problems, are listed below:

Stalking
Growling
Hissing
Scratching
Spraying
Fighting
Ambushing
Staring
Charging
Biting

THE SPLIT PERSONALITY

The funniest thing about Louie, was that he seemed to have this ability to suddenly transform himself into a completely different cat at times. One minute he'd be a big ol' grouch and give you that *look* when you wanted to come over and pet him. The next minute he would be up on the sink giving you that sweet little meow you seldom ever heard, unless he wanted a fresh drink of water from the kitchen faucet.

6

What really blew my mind once, was when we were at one of Louie's' veterinary appointments and he slashed a guy who thought he had been given the friendly "go ahead". He stuck his hand in the carrier to pet Louie and came back with a bloody finger... Louie had fooled him by luring him in with his sweet little deceptive looks!

KITTY MAY BE IN PHYSICAL PAIN

If you are unable to take your cat to the vet anytime soon, there are a few ways you can figure out if your cat is in some kind of pain. If you are even *able* to touch your cat at all, start from one end of his body and work your way to the other end by gently touching one area of his body at a time. Don't skip over anything, and observe his body language or reactions with each touch.

THINGS THAT COULD BE AILING YOUR CAT

- Abscess (infection under the skin).
- Arthritis, achy joints (in older cats).
- Constipation or hairball problem.
- Something is stuck in his paw.
- He has a toothache, or ear infection.
- Someone/something is bruising him.
- He may have a **U**rinary **T**ract **I**nfection.
- He might have impacted anal glands.
- If overweight, he may have back pain.
- He may actually be blind or deaf.

If your cat does not appear to have any physical problems, then consider the possibility that PTSD could be a likelihood. Look for *bad associations*. For instance, if you pick up a broom (for sweeping of course) does kitty act up? Or how about when you wear your big brown boots? Does your cat seem to hate them? He may have been traumatized by someone with a broom -- or by someone who was stepping on his tail in the past. If this is the case, whenever the "trigger" is present, he remembers that something bad may happen again.

STRESS, AND POST TRAUMA

Your cat's problem may not be physical. Cats can get pretty messed up emotionally, and you may not even be aware of it. Have you moved recently? Have you brought a new person or animal into the house? Has something major changed on the home front? Has kitty had kittens? Did you get her a new playmate? Has a new neighbor come along and brought a big dog or tomcat with them?

Sometimes an elusive animal may be lurking around your property at night and *you* won't know about it, but your cat *will*. A very common cause of bad behavior is due to territorial issues. Male cats (and even females) need an area to claim as their own, and if they do not have that, they are sure to act out, especially if they are already the temperamental type.

HEALTH CARE FOR A MEAN CAT

Treating an aggressive cat is extremely difficult and should be done at the vet, even if it is just for flea prevention. Trying to get a mean cat to cooperate while you attempt to get a pill down his throat is not fun. Unfortunately, some people might give up and just let it go because they're either afraid of the cat, or they're afraid of hurting him by using a little force to give him medicine. Call some vets or ask your friends if they know of a veterinarian who actually has experience with *wild (feral)* cats. The way I see it, if they can handle a completely wild cat, they can handle a grouchy domesticated cat. If you need to get your cat into a carrier, consider the following suggestions for handling him at home, so you can get him safely to the vet:

- Never yell, or make loud sounds to try and gain control.

- Never pull his tail to drag him out from under something.

- If you can grab the loose skin behind his neck, do it cautiously. Use your other hand to secure his back legs.

- Hold him close to you, don't leave him "dangling".

- If you do not have a carrier, use another container.

- It is imperative you do not allow him to be free in the car.

- Try to throw a thick towel on top of him and quickly scoop him up so that you can get him into the container.

- When you get him into the car, cover the carrier so that he can't see out at the traffic. This will prevent further stress.

If you're like I was when I had Louie, you don't have a lot money for vet care. I would absolutely never condone denying a cat of vet care. I do believe, however, that if you bring a lost, hungry kitten into your home, you *are* helping him, perhaps even saving his life. If you can't go to the vet for a couple of weeks, you can still take care of the cat to the best of your ability in the meantime. If you are on a tight budget, please do not put him back out on the streets, or give him to an over-crowded shelter. There are hundreds of people on the Internet or even in your circle of friends and family who may know about some home remedies you can use if he appears to be feeling ill. Of course, be prepared to hear some people say that it's dangerous to do this. To an immense degree, they are correct. There are some things you *can* do at home though, that have been proven safe. Just do the research, and verify your information with at least three different sources, and by all means, call a vet.

THE SPAY & NEUTER LECTURE

You've heard it over and over again and you're sick of it.. or you don't believe in having your cat "fixed". I'm not going to give you a hard time about having it done, although I highly recommend it, for everyone's sake. Neutered males have a built-in biological compulsion to go out and make babies. If they are living indoors, they may be peeing around windows and trying to get out of the house every time the door opens. They don't hate you or want to tick you off. They just have a strong need to get out and mate and they will mark their territory to let other males know that this is his mating ground, indoors and out.

It is unfortunate that neutering is so expensive and there are still too few organizations to help with the cost for low-income families. The struggling households need assistance more than any other, due to the fact that they can barely afford any cat supplies. Some people like to say, "if you can't pay the vet, don't get the pet." In my opinion, to do *anything at all* for a lost cat, is better than doing nothing. Giving a cat refuge is a kind act.

DON'T TOUCH ME LIKE THAT

Ask yourself why you got a cat. Many of us would say it was because we wanted someone to snuggle. Well, what if the cat you picked out is not a snuggler? What if he doesn't like to be handled all the time? Like people, cats actually have different preferences. For instance, my cat "Sugar" doesn't like to be pet on her belly. She likes to be rubbed gently across her cheeks and on top of her head. My other cat "Lucy" does not like to be touched on her back legs -you get the picture. Louie, well… he is the one who inspired me to write this book so needless to say, he would have a cow if you tried to touch him in *any* possible way. Bottom line is, touch your cat according to the reactions you get from him, by using various approaches. In the case of a *mean* cat, it is possible that he has some major *trust* issues. If he was bullied or mishandled by his previous owner, he is most likely apprehensive, and constantly on the defensive. Just pay close attention to what's setting him off, and avoid areas of his body that seem to be "off limits"

KITTY BACKGROUND CHECK

Chances are that you don't have any idea what your cat's life was like before he adopted you. You may have found him in a pet store or bought him from a breeder. Maybe he just "showed up" in your life. As great as it would be to know your cat's history, it's not likely you'll ever find out, but if you could ask your neighbors, or perhaps the person who raised him as a tiny kitten before giving him to you, "was he ever treated badly by anyone… or by another animal?" "Did he sustain any injuries that may not be visible at this time?" Ask if he was fed anything aside from mother's milk or kitten food. Find out if he grew up outdoors, or during severe weather.

LOUIE was actually *born* mean, or so *it seemed when we found him in a shed full of gargantuan insects, and extreme heat. I imagine if I had begun my life under those kinds of conditions, I would be grouchy too. He had some kind of sores on his lower back, so I treated him with an ointment and he began to heal. He was a biter from day one. I fed him, burped him, and gave*

him everything I could but I didn't have money for him to go to the vet. Perhaps if I had, I could have "fixed" whatever had him tied up in knots, and helped him to live happier. He did pretty well, nonetheless. I think his meanness is what kept his little butt alive all those years when he was faced with the many challenges of being such a small cat, in a big scary world.

CAT BREED REQUIREMENTS

If you don't already know everything about your cat's breed, you should do some research. You'll be surprised to find out things like, Maine Coons are fascinated with water... or that Siamese cats are very talkative and should not be scolded for being too vocal.

If you don't know your cat's breed, just look at him very closely for clues about what his natural tendencies might be. Does he have "kangaroo" legs? If so, he may be a naturally athletic cat. You should provide what he needs for climbing around, and enjoying a large running area.

Finding out what peaks your cat's natural interest will go a long way in helping him to feel like the world is right again. He won't feel like the proverbial fish out of water if he is given what is closest to his natural environment.

TERRITORY IS A BIG DEAL

Whether or not your cats coexists with other pets in your home, they each need to "own" an area. Males are especially in need of having their own territory. They need a high perch so that they can watch for prey, predators, or competitors. They often prefer to be near their human friend, or to at least be near something that holds their scent --but they also need a great deal of independence, and to not be *too needy of their owner*.

They like to rub their cheeks on things in the area they are trying to claim as their own. Pay attention to where they are doing this, and where they are spraying. Use this observation to determine where to set up their "world".

Nine times out of ten, the reason a cat is hostile is because of a *territorial uncertainty*. Even when your cat is indoors, he needs to feel as though he is the king of the whole neighborhood. This is especially true if there is another animal coming around and he feels that he, or his domain is under some kind of threat. It is an insecurity.

Territory to a cat is like a home and a yard is to *you*. Wouldn't you get agitated if you saw someone jumping your fence and trampling through your yard? How about someone *urinating on your car*? Your cat is just as ticked off about it as you are... think about that for a minute.

WALK A DOG, PLAY A CAT

Playing with your cat is every bit as important as walking a dog. If you take anything at all from this book, please remember this. <u>Playing with a cat is important because it simulates what's missing in their life, especially if they are living indoors</u>. Even if your cat is allowed outdoors.. for all those birds he shouldn't have caught, and all the mice he once tortured, he needs to get that same satisfaction some other way. He needs to hunt, so a moving toy is best. You could tie a fake bird, mouse, or bug to some fishing line or yarn and you'll be surprised at how fun it is for both you and the cat. If you're tired, or don't have time, get toys that move on their own, but are not loud.

As with walking a dog, your cat's play-time should be part of a routine. He should play (hunt), torture his catch for a few minutes, plop down on the floor and wait for you to bring him his real dinner --and then go to bed.

It is the night-time feeding with which you should include *wet* food, so that he feels like he's eating his kill. Dry food just doesn't cut it after hunting. He may just as well have been hunting for dried up old bones! I like to put some dry kibble next to his wet food so that he can have both. The dry food is good for his teeth and he should have it.

Next, he needs to have his own personal bed. Preferably one with a plush blanky, your scent nearby, and no visual stimulation. If he see's things moving around, he might be tempted to get up again. If you're trying to get the "nocturnal" out of him, you should keep things very still.

As you know, cats are, by nature, nocturnal, so don't expect him to sleep all night until you have made some adjustments. If he will not sleep all night , provide him with things that he can figure out on his own, to keep him busy while you are sleeping. If he insists on sleeping with you (or vice-versa), there should be a separate cat bed nearby that he can claim. If you have multiple cats, there should be one bed for each, and you should encourage them to use their bed, not yours.

In the morning, make time to play again, just a little bit before breakfast. This way, you have satisfied him enough to keep him out of your hair until you have more time to spend with him later in the day. He will probably sleep in the daytime, if he is feeling happy and secure. If you come home to find that he has chewed on things, or soiled the carpet, you need to evaluate the possible reasons and consider building him a sanctuary that allows him some outdoor time.

THE CATIO CONCEPT

In my opinion, an enclosed indoor/outdoor kitty sanctuary is the ideal solution for calming a mean cat. It is my hope that you and your cat live in a home with at least one small yard. If not, then consider everything on the following list, and scale it down to the miniature version. Here's what you should provide in the enclosure:

- Cat Grass and Catnip Garden
- Dirt Pad, Preferably Packed Down
- Pine/Cypress Mulch (nature's potty)
- Large Tree Limbs or Wooden Planks
- Multiple Perches, or Look-Out Towers
- Hanging Feather Toys, and Fake Prey.
- Fresh Water (Food Stays Indoors!)
- Little Hide Outs or Weather Shelters

The layout of the enclosure (or "catio" if you prefer) should be as tall as your surroundings (and landlord) will allow. It should include more than one pet door, (especially if you have more than one pet). If you have only one entrance/exit, there may be some guarding by at least one of the cats, and conflicts may arise. There should always be an "escape" route for all.

Prepare the shelters for the most severe weather conditions, in case kitty get's locked out by accident. The shelters should be warm in the winter, and cool in the summer. You can put heating pads down in the winter and they will love you even more for that! You should have equal amounts of shade and sun exposure. The limbs and planks should be staggered in an upwards and then downwards arrangement.

If you really want to help your cat get his mind off of biting people, get him some feeder crickets from the pet store! And the dirt pad I mentioned earlier? Unless your cat needs to impress someone, let him roll around on the dirt. He will love it! I have no idea *why*, but every single cat I've ever had does this and it's almost like giving them catnip! It just makes them happy so I don't care if they get dirty. I think they might be dressing in "camo" and it's really funny to see them like that!

If you are living in a really small place with a lot of rules, you can still put together a kitty-friendly perch by the window, or out on the patio… hence the name, "catio". I can almost guarantee that if you build this, and play with your cat routinely, your cat's horrible disposition will eventually fade away. You must allow some time for this to work though. Please do not give up after only a day or a week, as patience is indeed a virtue, and your entire family is worth every effort, and time needed for change.

Mean Cat by Melanie Gidget Adams

IS IT WORTH ALL THIS?

You might be thinking, "Why should I do all these things for a cat?" All you have to do is give the new plan a reasonable chance, and you will see "why". Someone can tell you to do "this", and to do "that", but they might leave out the most important thing for you to remember, *the reasons*. If your cat is happy, you are happy. If your cat is safe, you are safe in his presence. If he has his own space, he will give you back yours. If he has plenty to do, then he is not destroying your furniture, your relationships, or your belief in *change*.

Louie, in the "bush".

Mean Cat by Melanie Gidget Adams

EXAMPLES OF CAT FENCING

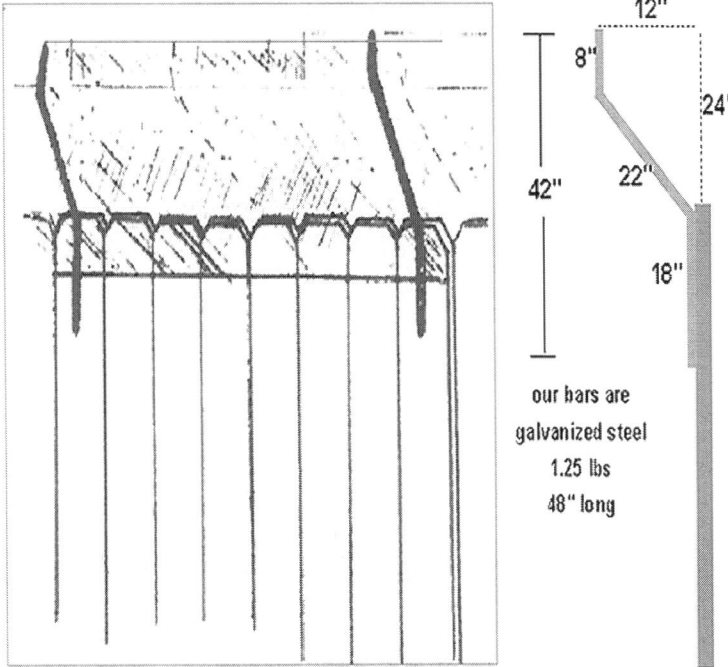

12"

8"

42"

22"

24'

18"

our bars are
galvanized steel
1.25 lbs
48" long

This design belongs to Affordable Cat Fence
For more about this system, please visit their website.

21

Mean Cat by Melanie Gidget Adams

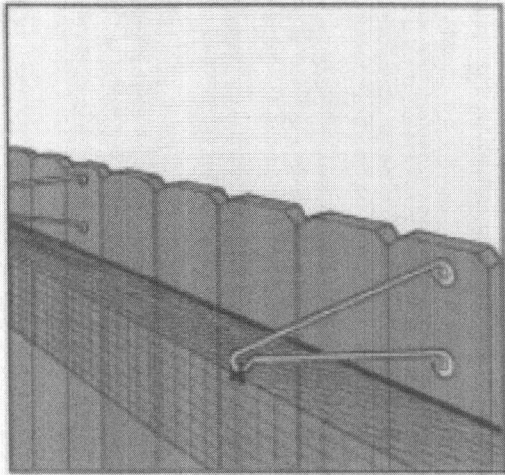

These two designs belong to Cat Fence-In.
Please visit their website for more information.

Mean Cat by Melanie Gidget Adams

This design belongs to PurrFectFence.
To learn more, please visit their website.

Mean Cat by Melanie Gidget Adams

This is a fence I built when I was on a tight budget. It's not tall, so I made the top it flimsy on purpose because most cats won't climb something if they think it's unstable. It worked well for my female cats, but not with the male (even though neutered). He was determined to go out.

Mean Cat by Melanie Gidget Adams

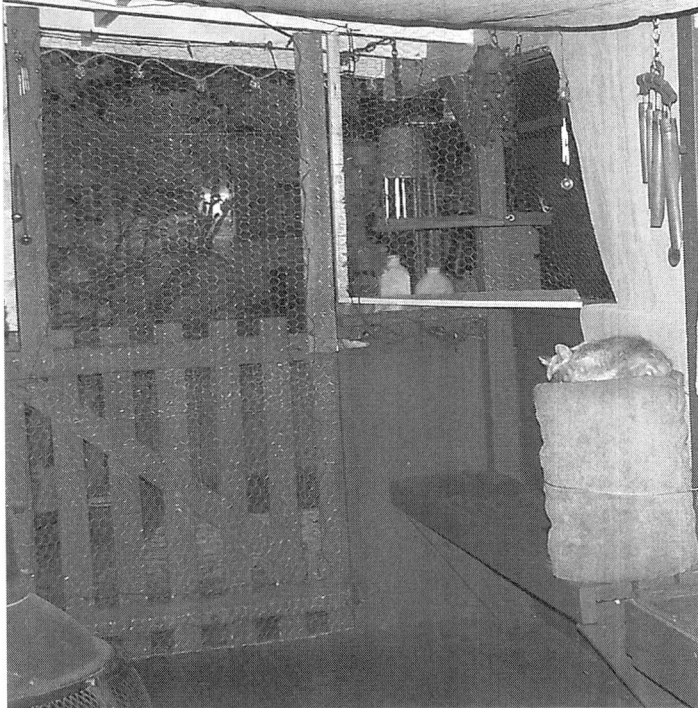

This design is my own, and it's a fenced-in deck.
I can almost say that it is full-proof because not only
do my cats never get out, they don't *want* to get out!
I can't, however, recommend it for *all* cat "personalities".

Mean Cat by Melanie Gidget Adams

GREAT CAT TOYS

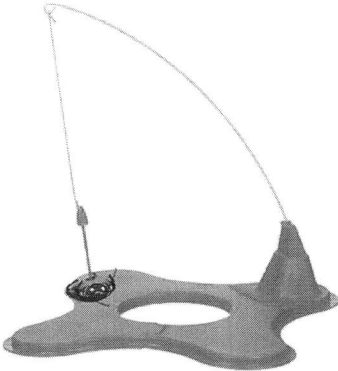

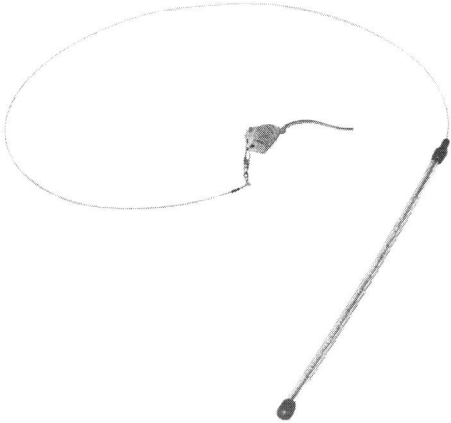

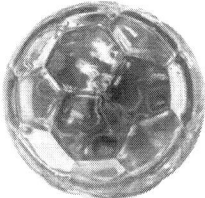

Mean Cat by Melanie Gidget Adams

2708066R00021

Printed in Great Britain
by Amazon.co.uk, Ltd.,
Marston Gate.